A.2 Informal learning in the music classroom

Most music teachers would place the motivation of their pupils high on their list of priorities, not only because motivation is an end in itself, but also because it is a prime building-block in the acquisition of musical skills and knowledge. Whilst motivating pupils during lessons is therefore a priority, teachers also want to make their lessons connect with the huge enjoyment that pupils get from music in their lives beyond the school.

Numerous attempts have been made to close the gap between pupils' own musical culture and that of the classroom. As teachers are well aware, popular music was first brought into schooling over three decades ago in attempts to connect with pupils' interests. However, whilst popular music today does form a major part of curriculum content, the informal learning practices of the musicians who create it have not generally been recognised or adopted as teaching and learning strategies within classrooms. Popular music itself may be present in most classrooms, but the ways in which it is created and passed on in the world outside school have been missing.

Informal music learning in the classroom aims to:

enhance pupil motivation, enjoyment and skill-acquisition in music lessons by tapping into the real-life learning practices of popular musicians

The project strategies have been trialled and evaluated mainly in Year 9 classrooms, and were designed with the 13-14 age-group in mind. However the principles at the core of the project could be adapted for a variety of educational environments and age groups.

CD-ROM guidance material
Please watch the introductory film for a general introduction to the project, and Film 5 'Reflections Year 9 Discussion' to see pupils discussing the project.

A.3 The five key principles (the centre of this approach

Many children, including young popular music become known as 'formal' and 'non-formal' i music, instrumental lessons, ensembles, band and beyond. However, at the heart of popular ..... transmission processes lie 'informal' learning practices, through which all popular musicians must pass in one way or another.

What do these informal learning practices involve, and in what respects do they differ from formal music education in the school?

Informal learning practices usually involve	Formal music education usually involves
Learning music which is personally chosen, familiar, and which the learners enjoy and strongly identify with.	Being introduced to music which is often new and unfamiliar, normally chosen by a teacher.
Learning by listening to recordings and copying them by ear.	Learning through notation or other written or verbal instructions.
Learning alongside friends through talking about music, peer-assessment, listening, watching and imitating each other, usually without adult supervision.	Learning through expert instruction, and receiving adult supervision.
Assimilating skills and knowledge in personal, often haphazard ways according to musical preferences, starting with 'whole', 'real-world' pieces of music.	Following a progression from simple to complex, often involving specially-composed music, a curriculum or a graded syllabus.
Maintaining a close integration of listening, performing, improvising and composing throughout the learning process.	Gradually specialising in and differentiating between listening, performing, improvising and composing skills; often tending to emphasise the reproductive more than the creative skills.

The five key principles are:

Principle 1   **Learning music that pupils choose, like and identify with**

Principle 2   **Learning by listening and copying recordings**

Principle 3   **Learning with friends**

Principle 4   **Personal, often haphazard learning without structured guidance**

Principle 5   **Integration of listening, performing, improvising and composing**

Each of the seven stages of the project draws on, and attempts to replicate as closely as possible, two or more of these five key principles.

A.4 Piloting the approach

The ideas behind the project derive from research undertaken for the book *How Popular Musicians Learn: A Way Ahead For Music Education* (Lucy Green, Ashgate Publishers, 2002). One of the outcomes at the end of the book was a number of suggestions for incorporating informal learning into classroom and instrumental teaching strategies. This project has enabled some of the suggestions for classroom strategies to be put into practice, developed and evaluated.

The project's teaching and learning strategies have been enacted and evaluated in 21 secondary schools. This includes a pre-pilot school and three pilot schools in London, who participated in an initial study supported by the Esmée Fairbairn Foundation during 2003-04. The first year of the main study phase took place in four Hertfordshire schools during 2004-05. These are the four schools that are featured on the CD-ROM which is inside this resource pack. A further 13 Hertfordshire schools then joined the project in September 2005.

The recommendations and findings below are based on our observations, field notes and audio recordings of pupils at work, and on extensive consultation with the pupils and teachers who participated in the study. All the teachers have read and approved this pack.[1]

A.5 Using this resource

The pack is based on what has happened in the project schools to date. It suggests ways for the classroom teacher to adopt and adapt informal learning practices within the formal setting of the classroom. It gives details of the teaching and learning strategies for seven separate stages of the project, with a brief overview of the main results, and illustrative quotes from teachers and pupils in the three pilot schools and the first four main study schools. The enclosed audio-CDs and Section Resources provide all the additional teaching materials.

A5.1 The CD-ROM

The enclosed CD-ROM provides documentary films of the project as it unfolded in the four main study schools. It also contains audio samples of work produced by pupils in those four schools and in three of the pilot schools.

The schools in the documentary films had additional funding for instruments *(for details please see A7.3 Equipment)*. However it is important to stress that the pilot schools and some of the remaining main study schools put the strategies into action using only their usual set of classroom instruments, mainly electric keyboards and hand percussion instruments.

A5.2 The order of the stages

It is essential to begin with Stages 1 and 2, but there is flexibility thereafter for teachers to develop the strategies in their own ways, and if desired, to integrate the ideas presented here with more formal classroom work.

> Teachers may wish to develop their own materials to complement or supplement those provided here.

A6 What does the project involve?
A6.1 The role of the teacher

The role of the teacher is perhaps the most interesting as well as the most challenging aspect of the project.

In the first lesson of each stage pupils are given a task by the teacher. Throughout each stage, resources are organised by the teacher; ground rules, such as respect for instruments, staff and other pupils, are laid down and maintained by the teacher; and in all similar respects the teacher's role is no different from what would normally be expected in any classroom. But aside from the above, pupils are free to approach the task, and to organise themselves within their groups, in whatever ways they wish, setting their own objectives and steering their own course through learning.

Summary of the role of the teacher in the informal music classroom:
- **set the task going**
- **stand back**
- **observe**
- **diagnose**
- **guide**
- **suggest**
- **model**
- **take on pupils' perspectives**
- **help pupils achieve the objectives they set for themselves**

For an illustration of the role of the teacher in practice, please see pages 12 - 14.

A6.2 The seven project stages

The project is organised in seven stages. Each stage takes place over a period of three to six lessons. The exact length of each stage is up to a teacher's judgement and preference, and will vary from school to school. In the project schools the length of each stage varied from three weeks at the least to six weeks at the most, with lesson lengths ranging from 50 to 90 minutes. In all but two cases lessons were weekly; in the remaining two cases they were fortnightly. The findings and recommendations are based upon following the seven stages in the given order. Some teachers may consider changing the order of the stages, or omitting some stages altogether. Some or all of the latter stages may be omitted without affecting the essence of the project.

The first two stages contain the main ingredients and core activities of the approach. They will affect how pupils approach the latter stages. Therefore these two stages must come first, if the project is to be put into action.

The core of the approach lies in Stages 1 and 2

Each stage is not a module within a scheme of work. Rather, each stage represents an approach to teaching and learning, drawn from the real-life practices of musicians in the informal sphere.

A6.3 Progression

Each stage contains progression within itself and builds progressively on previous ones. The nature of the progression is implicit, but observable, based on growth in pupils' experiences of themselves as musicians.

Year 9 pupils' comments	Teachers' comments
'Because it was really hard getting it all together, when we actually performed to the class we were all really proud of ourselves.' 'This gives you the chance to prove what you're capable of.'	'What we've done with the stages has been a natural progression with the pupils' interests in mind — going with what they would want first. Just letting them have a go and then with a bit of guidance letting them have another go.'

A6.4 Differentiation

Differentiation is by outcome. Pupils choose for themselves, and organise for each other within their groups, tasks that suit different individuals' abilities.

Year 9 pupils' comments	Teachers' comments
'We've got used to each others' different style of playing — now we know everyone's ability we know what they can do.' 'We just like chose a part that would like fit our abilities, so like if we were good we would play something that was quite difficult, but if we weren't as good we'd just play something that was quite easy.'	'Regardless of their ability this is something that everybody can succeed in at their own level because they're making their own choices about what they play, and with a bit of input from us to help them find a drum beat or a chord pattern it is possible for them all to access this at their own level.'

A6.5 Involvement of all pupils

Many pupils who had not previously excelled or cooperated in music classes surprised their teachers by showing themselves to be able and willing musicians, or to possess previously hidden leadership qualities.

Year 9 pupils' comments	Teachers' comments
'I think my behaviour grade has gone up. Because like when you're in the classroom just doing like written and stuff, you get bored and you just muck around and stuff. But when you're doing this you can't get bored.' 'Last year when we were sitting in the classroom, there are people in your group who are like naughty and they always get told off. But this time because you're on your own, with your friends, you just get on with it and you do it how you want to.'	'I was completely gob-smacked to see Scott singing in front of the whole class. I wouldn't have got that. I mean, I've got boys in my choir, but, you know, they're not that kind of Year 9 kid who will just not have a care and just sing. We were really thrilled with that actually. I was really thrilled with the girls as well just singing.' 'I think they feel very equal actually, because they're, it's not a case of "oh, you're good at music" or whatever — they feel quite on a par with each other so that's good.'

Some individual pupils tend to spend time sitting and watching, especially during the early stages. Learning by listening and watching peers is a central informal learning practice and forms part of one of the five key principles on which the project is based. Our experience suggests that as time goes by these pupils become increasingly active and involved through their own motivation and through the co-operation and encouragement of other group members.

> "We were kind of silly at first and then we realised by ourselves that we had to get on with it."
> Year 9 pupil

A6.6 Size of groups

The smallest group in any of the project schools had only one pupil, a girl who preferred to work on her own for the first two stages of the project. The largest group was eight. In both these cases the strategies were considered successful by the teachers. However our recommendation for an ideal situation would be to have groups of three to six.

A6.7 Friendship groups

Many pupils stated that being allowed to work in friendship groups was a major motivational factor as well as an aid to group cooperation.

Year 9 pupils' comments	Teachers' comments
'We got to like pick our groups at the start so we could work with people that we knew we could get on with.' 'I'm really pleased because of like what we can do…It's all about teamwork.' '…when you're not with your friends, like, and when you're with other people you don't really like, you're like always arguing and it wastes time.'	'It's about giving them space to create their group ethos before they start, and working in friendship groups and just being prepared to trust them.' 'The pupils can decide their own learning and if one pupil is struggling in one particular aspect, another pupil can actually help them out.'

A6.8 Group cooperation

All the teachers agreed that group cooperation was higher than expected, and many pupils saw cooperation as a learning outcome.

Year 9 pupils' comments	Teachers' comments
'I think I've learnt to, like, work more as a team, like listen to each other, whereas before like I used to like always be speaking over everyone kind of thing, but I've like got used to working as a group now better.' 'We like helped each other and everything. We like took, every week we'd help each other on different instruments.'	'They worked brilliantly as groups. They cooperated, they were all contributing as well, so their work had a sense of purpose – they were all working towards creating a good performance.'

A6.9 Motivation

The teachers were unanimous that motivation and enjoyment have been exceptionally high throughout the project, and this was also echoed in pupils' words.

Year 9 pupils' comments	Teachers' comments
'I thought it was good, it was fun, it was a challenge and I enjoyed it, I really enjoyed it.' 'I think I might take music next year, because this has kind of convinced me to.' 'This way we can actually learn about music.'	'I think it really works in terms of the motivation of the students, of their enthusiasm, and it actually has had effects on the behaviour of students too. So I've seen really marked improvements in how many students stay on task, how you can actually leave students in a room, with instruments and they will do the work that they are expected to do.'

Situation	Don't	Do
A group of pupils have chosen to copy a song which you think is much too hard for them; one of the other songs on their CD would have been more approachable.	Tell them they shouldn't do the difficult song and insist they work on the other one.	Say nothing about their choice of song. It is very important that pupils are free to make their own choices. By trying the copying task they will gradually learn to make more suitable choices for themselves.
A pupil is attempting to play a difficult melody on the keyboard.	'Model' the melody part yourself, using a simplified version if it seems appropriate, showing the pupil where the notes are; then leave the pupil on their own to continue working on the part. They are then able to accept your advice or reject it based on their own decisions
A pupil who has never played the bass guitar before is holding the instrument flat on their lap, making it difficult to depress the strings.	Tell the pupil that what they are attempting is too difficult for them, and devise a simpler part for them to play. Stand over them to ensure they get it right.	Nothing at first. Allow the pupil to experiment in their own way with holding the instrument. After some time, perhaps even two lessons later, when you feel the pupil is receptive, suggest they might find it easier if they hold the instrument differently. Show them how, and then leave the room.
	Tell the pupil they are holding the instrument incorrectly, show them how to hold it correctly, and insist that they maintain that hold.	
Four boys with behaviour problems have grouped themselves together as a friendship group.	Insist that they are not able to work together and move them into other groups.	Give them some time to work alone, showing that you trust them to work independently. If they are struggling to organise themselves ask 'which one of you would like to play the rhythm?' of their chosen song (for example), and then model the rhythm for them, hopefully engaging one pupil, who will later start to organise his peers.
Pupils are unable to decide what instruments to play, as they maintain that none of them are good at music.	Assign instruments to them and give them basic notes to play on these instruments.	Start by discussing with the pupils their own musical interests, whether any of them sing in an informal way outside of school. Encourage them to try different instruments, and reassure them that this project is about the learning process, not necessarily about how good they are at the end of it. Perhaps model some notes from the pupils' chosen song on different instruments, then leave the pupils to experiment themselves before offering further guidance.
Pupils are all playing their parts and are not listening to each other, and have been doing this most of the time for two lessons.	Tell the pupils to put down their instruments and listen to you, and organise the pupils yourself. Stay in the room to make sure they have listened to your advice.	Spend a few minutes in the room listening to the pupils' work and observing their behaviour, and then quietly approach one member of the group (for example the drummer) and suggest that they take the lead in the group and organise their peers. Encourage them to discuss what is important when in a band (i.e. communication and listening to one another), and make a few suggestions as to how they could rehearse their piece together. Then leave the room and allow the pupils time to absorb your suggestion.

Project Stage 7

Stage description	Pupils listen to, discuss and select a piece of classical music drawn from the core of the classical canon, including regions that are likely to be unfamiliar to pupils. They are provided with a recording of the music in its original form, and broken down into separate melody and bass lines. Pupils listen to, discuss, select, aurally copy, rehearse and perform the music.
National Curriculum mapping	• Pupils further develop vocal and instrumental skills (1a/1b). They perform with increasing control of instrument specific techniques (1b). They practise, rehearse and perform with awareness of different parts, the role and contribution of different members of the group, and the audience and venue (1c). • Pupils improvise their own versions of their chosen piece of music, exploring and developing musical ideas when performing (2a). They produce, develop and extend musical ideas, selecting and combining resources within musical structures and the given genre, style and tradition (2b). • Pupils analyse, evaluate and compare pieces of music (3a). They communicate ideas and feelings about music using expressive language and musical vocabulary to justify their own opinions (3b). They adapt the musical ideas, and refine and improve their own and others' work (3c). • Pupils listen with discrimination and internalise and recall sounds (4a). They identify the expressive use of musical elements, devices, tonalities and structures (4b). They identify the resources, conventions, processes and procedures used in the selected musical genre, style and tradition (4c). They identify the contextual influences that affect the way music is created, performed and heard (4d).
NC criteria satisfied	1a / 1b / 1c / 2a / 2b / 3a / 3b / 3c / 4a / 4b / 4c / 4d

Project Overview

Stage description	General overview of project.
National Curriculum mapping	• Pupils complete a range of musical activities that integrate performing, composing, listening and appraising (5a). They respond to a range of musical starting points (5b). They work independently and in groups (5c). Pupils are able to use ICT to create, manipulate and refine sounds (5d). They gain knowledge, skills and understanding through a range of live and recorded music from different times and cultures including music from the British Isles, the Western classical tradition, folk, jazz and popular genres (5e).
NC criteria satisfied	5a / 5b / 5c / 5d / 5e

Project Stage 4 / 5	
Stage description	Building on the knowledge, skills and understanding developed during Stages 1, 2 and 3, pupils compose, rehearse and perform their own music in groups. They receive guidance from musical role models – either external musicians or other musicians from within the school.
National Curriculum mapping	• Pupils develop vocal techniques and sing with musical expression (1a). They perform with increasing control of instrument specific techniques (1b). They practise, rehearse and perform with awareness of different parts, the roles and contribution of the different members of the group, and the audience and venue (1c). • Pupils improvise their own musical ideas, exploring and developing these when performing and rehearsing (2a). They produce, develop and extend their own musical ideas, selecting and combining musical resources within musical structures, genres, styles and traditions (2b). • Pupils analyse, evaluate and compare pieces of music, including their own (3a). They communicate ideas and feelings about music using expressive language and musical vocabulary to justify their own opinions (3b). They adapt their own musical ideas, and refine and improve their own and others' work (3c). • Pupils listen with discrimination to internalise and recall sounds (4a). They identify the expressive use of musical elements, devices, tonalities and structures (4b). They identify the resources, conventions, processes and procedures, including use of ICT, and relevant notations used in their selected musical genre, style and tradition (4c). They identify the contextual influences that affect the way music is created, performed and heard (4d).
NC criteria satisfied	1a / 1b / 1c / 2a / 2b / 3a / 3b / 3c / 4a / 4b / 4c / 4d

Project Stage 6	
Stage description	Pupils listen to, discuss and select a piece of classical music from a selection of pieces used on current TV advertisements. They listen to, discuss, select, aurally copy, rehearse and perform the music. They direct their own route through learning, individually and as a group.
National Curriculum mapping	• Pupils further develop vocal and instrumental skills (1a/1b). They perform with increasing control of instrument specific techniques (1b). They practise, rehearse and perform with awareness of different parts, the role and contribution of different members of the group, and the audience and venue (1c). • Pupils improvise their own versions of their chosen piece of music, exploring and developing musical ideas when performing (2a). They produce, develop and extend musical ideas, selecting and combining resources within musical structures and the given genre, style and tradition (2b). • Pupils analyse, evaluate and compare pieces of music (3a). They communicate ideas and feelings about music using expressive language and musical vocabulary to justify their own opinions (3b). They adapt the musical ideas, and refine and improve their own and others' work (3c). • Pupils listen with discrimination and internalise and recall sounds (4a). They identify the expressive use of musical elements, devices, tonalities and structures (4b). They identify the resources, conventions, processes and procedures used in the selected musical genre, style and tradition (4c). They identify the contextual influences that affect the way music is created, performed and heard (4d).
NC criteria satisfied	1a / 1b / 1c / 2a / 2b / 3a / 3b / 3c / 4a / 4b / 4c / 4d

Project Stage 2

Stage description	Pupils are provided with a recording of Cameo's 'Word Up' on a CD which contains two versions of the complete song, plus 15 riffs played separately and in combination. Pupils listen, discuss, select and aurally copy the riffs vocally and instrumentally in order to create their own version of the song.
National Curriculum mapping	• Pupils further develop vocal and instrumental skills (1a/1b). They perform with increasing control of instrument specific techniques (1b). They practise, rehearse and perform with awareness of different parts, the roles and contribution of the different members of the group, and the audience and venue (1c). • Pupils improvise and explore musical ideas when performing and rehearsing (2a). They develop and extend musical ideas, selecting and combining resources within musical structures and the given genre, style and tradition (2b). • Pupils analyse and evaluate a piece of music (3a). They communicate ideas and feelings about music using expressive language and musical vocabulary to justify their own opinions (3b). They adapt their own musical ideas, and refine and improve their own and others' work. (3c). • Pupils listen with discrimination to internalise and recall sounds (4a). They identify the expressive use of musical elements, devices and structures (4b). They identify resources, conventions, processes and procedures, including the use of relevant notations, used in the selected musical genre, style and tradition (4c). They identify the contextual influences that affect the way music is created, performed and heard (4d).
NC criteria satisfied	1a / 1b / 1c / 2a / 2b / 3a / 3b / 3c / 4a / 4b / 4c / 4d

Project Stage 3

Stage description	Building on the knowledge, skills and understanding developed during Stages 1 and 2, pupils have a second opportunity to listen, discuss, select, aurally copy, rehearse and perform music, as with Stage 1.
National Curriculum mapping	• Pupils further develop vocal and instrumental skills (1a/1b). They perform with increasing control of instrument specific techniques (1b). They practise, rehearse and perform with awareness of different parts, the roles and contribution of the different members of the group, and the audience and venue (1c). • Pupils improvise their own versions of their chosen song, exploring and developing musical ideas when performing (2a). They produce, develop and extend musical ideas, selecting and combining resources within the musical structures of their chosen song (2b). • Pupils analyse, evaluate and compare pieces of music (3a). They communicate ideas and feelings about music using expressive language and musical vocabulary to justify their own opinions (3b). They adapt their own musical ideas and refine and improve their own and others' work (3c). • Pupils listen with discrimination and internalise and recall sounds (4a). They identify the expressive use of musical elements, devices and structures (4b). They identify the contextual influences that affect the way music is created, performed and heard (4d).
NC criteria satisfied	1a / 1b / 1c / 2a / 2b / 3a / 3b / 3c / 4a / 4b / 4d

A6.12 Assessment, the National Curriculum and Government requirements

Teachers who took part in the project have agreed unanimously that National Curriculum assessment criteria, attainment targets and their usual methods of assessment could be applied to the strategies. The QCA, through its Music Development Group, has been kept informed about the project since its inception, and has advised that the informal learning strategies are consistent with, and help meet, the requirements for performing, composing and appraising in the National Curriculum at Key Stage 3.

One participating school had an Ofsted inspection while a Musical Futures project lesson was taking place. The ensuing report contained the following:

See the following tables for how this guide matches with the National Curriculum criteria.

> 'Pupils' achievements in a number of special activities, such as Musical Futures, are very good or excellent... The project is designed to investigate how pupils can take control of their own learning, and addresses the low take-up of music nationally after Year 9.
> It demonstrated high motivation and very good progress in lessons.'
>
> Taken from Inspection Report 268909, Sheredes School, Hoddesdon, February / March 2005.

Project Stage 1	
Stage description	Pupils emulate the real-life learning practices of young, beginner popular musicians, by listening, discussing, selecting, aurally-copying, rehearsing, arranging and performing their own choice of music. They direct their own route through learning, individually and as a group.
National Curriculum mapping	• Pupils develop vocal and instrumental skills (1a/1b). They perform with increasing control of instrument specific techniques (1b). They practise, rehearse and perform with awareness of different parts, the roles and contribution of the different members of the group, and the audience and venue (1c). • Pupils improvise their own versions of their chosen song, exploring and developing musical ideas when performing (2a). They produce, develop and extend musical ideas, selecting and combining resources within the musical structures of their chosen song (2b). • Pupils analyse, evaluate and compare pieces of music (3a). They communicate ideas and feelings about music using expressive language and musical vocabulary to justify their own opinions (3b). They adapt their own musical ideas and refine and improve their own and others' work (3c). • Pupils listen with discrimination and internalise and recall sounds (4a). They identify the expressive use of musical elements, devices and structures (4b). They identify the contextual influences that affect the way music is created, performed and heard (4d).
NC criteria satisfied	1a / 1b / 1c / 2a / 2b / 3a / 3b / 3c / 4a / 4b / 4d

A6.10 Group performances during the lesson

Some lessons included group performances and class discussions of them. This is recommended and is entirely within the rationale of the project, since peer-assessment through listening to and watching each other are central parts of informal learning practices.

> **Teaching Tip**
> Rather than getting the whole class back into the main classroom for the group performances, in many project-schools the 'audience' went around the practice spaces to listen to others. This often meant that the audience stood in a doorway or outside a practice space to listen. Teachers agreed that the system worked well, as it minimised time spent setting up equipment, and enabled pupils to perform in the space to which they were accustomed.

In some of the project schools teachers made videos of pupils performing in their practice spaces, and then followed this up with a whole class viewing and discussion of the video. Teachers also experimented with recording the pupils and playing back the recordings to the whole class, followed by a discussion of the performances.

A6.11 Lesson structure

The structure of each lesson is relatively free, and in some lessons pupils spend the entire time working in small groups.

Year 9 pupils' comments

'It's nice to just have, like, a blank space of time.'

'Can't we just come in and get on with it? We know exactly what we need to do, we don't need reminding of it.'

Teachers' comments

'I've learnt that things don't just last a lesson. I'm very quick paced when I do things, and sometimes if I see one person off task I will stop it and bring everybody in 'cause I want everyone to be focused the whole time. And maybe I'm stopping people from developing further by not giving them that time.'

'It takes them a few weeks to actually build the confidence to attempt things, and I find that pupils need the consistency to feel confident in what they're doing. And if it takes a couple of weeks of being with the same instruments, with the same group, with the same CD to actually build that confidence, I think it's really important that we allow for it.'

'As teachers we're always working to a really tight timescale, and to lesson objectives, every lesson must be this structured thing, and I don't think we really give them the space to explore actually working as groups and doing those things. And then when it does come together then they do get the motivation from actually having achieved something. But I didn't realise that before — I'm only starting to realise that now.'

'With the five-part lesson plan I can actually justify why I don't want to do it, or why I want instead to stretch my five-part lesson over three weeks.'

> ❞I think my behaviour grade has gone up. Because like when you're in the classroom just doing like written and stuff, you get bored and you just muck around and stuff. But when you're doing this you can't get bored.❞
>
> Year 9 pupil